Precedented Parroting

Precedented
Parroting

Barbara Tran

Palimpsest Press
1171 Eastlawn Ave.
Windsor, Ontario. N8S 3J1
www.palimpsestpress.ca

Printed and bound in Canada
Cover design and book typography by Ellie Hastings
Edited by Jim Johnstone

Palimpsest Press would like to thank the Canada Council for the Arts
and the Ontario Arts Council for their support of our publishing
program. We also acknowledge the assistance of the Government of
Ontario through the Ontario Book Publishing Tax Credit.

A Anstruther Books

Canada Council   Conseil des Arts
for the Arts   du Canada

ONTARIO ARTS COUNCIL
CONSEIL DES ARTS DE L'ONTARIO
an Ontario government agency
un organisme du gouvernement de l'Ontario

ONTARIO | ONTARIO
CREATES | CRÉATIF

Canadä

LIBRARY AND ARCHIVES CANADA CATALOGUING IN PUBLICATION

TITLE: Precedented parroting / Barbara Tran.
NAMES: Tran, Barbara, author.
DESCRIPTION: Poems.
IDENTIFIERS: Canadiana (print) 20230568718
             Canadiana (ebook) 20230568726

ISBN 9781990293641 (SOFTCOVER)
ISBN 9781990293658 (EPUB)
SUBJECTS: LCGFT: Poetry.
CLASSIFICATION: LCC PS8639.R36 P74 2024 | DDC C811/.6—DC23

Contents

The sounds uttered by birds offer
in several respects the nearest analogy to language.
—Charles Darwin, *The Descent of Man*

A Music numerous as space –
But neighboring as Noon –

—Emily Dickinson
"The Birds begun at Four o'clock –"

"What colour?"

— Alex, African Grey Parrot
Upon being shown his reflection in a mirror

1

Raven Takes Wing

The first step is admitting it: I am a willful forgetter
                 (I've taken this step many times)

    My bones are inclined to forget
the crick in my neck
      the dull ache in my wrist

                It should be obvious how they got this way
                It is obvious

          somewhere   in the recesses
     Black drongo   common kingfisher
       I summon memories like birds

    I assign them colours
     If I admire the way they swoop

     and soar
dive and catch
    if I separate myself

        from them   make them
          pretty things

with wings
    things
        outside myself

                things   that sing   things
           that eat the bugs

that plague me
          I can both
      remember them

                  and send them
             scattering

Kite   cormorant
heron the colour
    of a pale amethyst

                If I think of them this way
      the way they move

   is not frightening
   the way they plunge
     and peck   the way they

    persist
      buoyed

by   a gust
I cannot see
       After Dionysus   set

          tigers   upon Amethystos
                he wept   his rage   trans-

      muted into wine-
    coloured tears
         that stained the girl

      Artemis had turned
    to stone   It's how amethysts

got their colour
      how   my memory
        the one I keep trying to send

              into flight
                was stained   Rage
         An apology

    The egret   a white flag
   Thin throat   Thin song

It's impossible to hear egret
          without

an echo

Regret   My thoughts
are scattering

like sandpipers
I am falling
out of reason   The birds

are losing their feathers
The wind

is forcing them
to land   They are waving
like flags

like surrender   like
egrets

feet planted
in thick
mud

Blue from a Distance

filoplume semiplume
  bristles
    an empty

calamus Feathers receive
  no nourishment They are
  dead

structures On a bird
  feather each barb
    holds smaller

barbs On us
  each loss
    encompasses smaller

losses Feathers soften
  the lines
    where different parts

of the body meet They sculpt
  the body
    into a teardrop

shape There is a phrase
  in Vietnamese chia buồn
    sharing sadness

In my family's case
  it's like Jesus
    with his two

fish and five
    loaves of bread A
    boundless

supply Except
    in our case it's salt
    on salt

sadness
    layered atop sorrow
    The calamus lies

beneath the skin
    The rachis holds
    two vanes A layer

of keratin
    allows space
    for light

to play Large
    tail feathers can act
    as a rudder help

with braking There is no
    blue pigment in bird
    feathers Blue feathers

are a result
    of structure reflection
    wavelengths

bouncing In Vietnamese
    there is no
    specific word

for blue It shares
   the same name
      as green To distinguish

you might say
   the xanh
      of leaves or xanh

as the sky
   which today
      is the furthest thing

   from blue

Buttercups in Foil on the Windowsill

She never set foot in that house,
was on the other side of the world, living
her life as if every day were Sunday, though
given her location this was no
blessing, just another day of
shortages, of thuds in the distance that made
one's mind leap even when one's
body was in bed. One day bled
into another, the ash of intention blowing
into oblivion. To accomplish
anything, one had to leap through
the doorway of existence, existence being
an opening that allowed all you love to leave
as easily as it arrived.

Loon Song

Fever puts a funny
halo around everything
until you can't tell sky

from slipper God
from the stuffed hedgehog
whose head your dog

hollowed out It's a good ego
booster: believing
you can soar

without even kicking
off the covers Caged
by fever I slump

on a pillow as flat
as the earth envisioned
by Herodotus its far end

draping over the edge
of the bed My feet
are an illusion the way a wet

parking lot can appear as a lake
to a loon
in flight My mind

a useless
appendage that flops
when it should flip

Loons' feet are set
way back making them agile
in water awkward

on land Like planes
they need a runway for takeoff
but a water one It can require

up to 400 metres of running
for them to ascend They can
become stranded

on a small pond
the way I am on this raft
of a bed

wishing to pass
those orphaned
in Atlanta a precise

motherless roadmap
We are inventive with
our torture Swinging

fists are so passé A swing
in a cage allows you to fly
all the way

to the bars grasp
them with your hands
or beak Glass

reflections give
the illusion
of space and delightful

company When challenged
with infection bees
will increase activity

to raise the temperature
of the hive V
was a lifelong

believer
in karma Fever
protects the way

madness does
With a swing
and a mirror

Feelings in A-Minor

White suburban sparrow
   plastic picket line
      flags stabbed into home fronts
It Depends Day

The neighbour's grass ever greener
   American Miss Dream
      40 acres and the moon my own
crescent moon question mark

Please
   pass the salted migrations
      It's a cactus of a time

Precedented Parroting

I.

It was many years ago that I read this
I could not forget it
Because I could not forget it I re-read it

They rock themselves to comfort
themselves They scream and suffer
from insomnia and nightmares

They attack
those who try to help They self-
mutilate At the sanctuary a war

veteran and a cockatoo The cockatoo
was kept in a kitchen
drawer All her life

in a drawer Kept there
by a
What would you call

The bird is
bald She plucks
her feathers Her skin

is reptilian
bleeding Parrots
call one another

by distinct sounds My name
means strange stranger
foreign The cockatoo

shares it Parrots
traumatized pace
and rock They mumble

to themselves I return
to these stories I've read before
I re-read

I pace and rock I murmur
to myself I no longer
have feathers

II.

1871 18 Chinese men and boys
   lynched They lived
      on a street not far from here in Los

Angeles 3 weeks ago
   in Brooklyn a woman
      on her own porch 2nd-

degree burns Face
   hands body Acid She is Asian
      American In Texas a 2-

year-old child
   stabbed Someone
      unhinged

over what
   someone else
      termed the *Chinese*

virus
   "birdbrained" "mindless mimicry" "mere
   parroting"

On a neighbourhood
   app someone offers
      paper towels seeks

bleach I offer
   a list of birds flora
      seek sleep

The cliffs here in Eagle Rock
are eroding
Ravens roving
Beyond
date palms

a four-legged, bushy-
tailed winged
creature pursued
by a raven My eye
could make

no sense   The wing-
span wide   the long
tail flicking   The four
legs digging   for footing
A second   tail

feathered   spread   A red-
tailed   hawk
talons
cradling
its catch

III.

I am red
and orange In my dream I have a blue
head I am outside

myself and inside
my blue head From inside
I can see   a tree orange

against a   fiery   red
background It is fall
mine the tree's the coast's

the earth's In my blue
head I am crashing
which means

I was flying

2

Một: Rooted

$$\left(\quad \begin{array}{l} \text{This is a family photo album} \\ \text{that contains} \\ \text{no photos} \end{array} \quad \right)$$

On the first page empty

photo corners   My mother hid
her swelling belly   Then

after I was born
hid me

I grew up
afraid of strangers And since

I was rarely taken out of the house
everyone—

except my mother
and siblings—

was a stranger This
is how it began

I'm good
at telling

how things begin
I'm not good

at telling
how things end   So I'll tell

only beginnings   Between
beginnings know

there are endings Many
endings

(   )

You should know ... I come from a family
of unreliable narrators

(Also thieves
though   arguably

these are the same)

We are not willfully deceptive
Rather we suffer from similar

whiteouts
Right not blackouts

We're conscious for these

33

Pregnant my mother carried a packet of salt
wherever she went In Church she would lick
a finger then press it to the fine white grains

Was she remembering her father and
a life lived according to the tides The sharp
bite of salt on the tip of her tongue Was hers

the pure, sea salt sadness of the outcast?

The question of who
the most reliable narrator
in the family is

is debatable

)

)

)

definition of home   rooted

If you can't say
                    country

without conjuring
                                   soil
            and sea

        water   reaching
                    between water
            spinach   stems

        can you ever *not*

be homesick?

What if you've never actually   been home?

3

In the beak
of a bird
is a sunflower

seed weight
or energy? Effort
in flight

increases with increases
in load Light
as a bent

feather
Refraction refers
to the bending

that occurs
between one medium
and another

Every memory
carries weight Pack
light Migration

may involve
arduous
treks across

metaphoric mountains
and through

~

atmospheric rivers
Note
the angle

of incidence Excessive
effort renders
some

fractious Fatigue eats
at the mind
before entering

the muscles Lyric
diversions
are for the hearty

and hale (Think
hummingbird)
Awareness

of the endpoint
increases perception
of effort You

are an oriole This
poem is a roadmap
writ

with anticipation
Destination
unknown

Knowing this

Do you
eat
or fly?

Red O

Red-tailed hawk Red
ring from a milk jug
encountered on the Mishe
Mokwa trail But it wasn't that plastic
piece of dread No The red
of someone's pony-
tail elastic something shed
as involuntarily as red
blood cells Maria
fatigued unknowing blaming
age I blamed some unknown
hiker careless I thought dropping
trash amidst the black
sage and juniper *Who*
drinks milk on a
hike I should have
thought but didn't stop
to think *No one*
No one drinks from a milk
jug on the trail
You'd have to lug
it sun needling
you plastic in your pack crushing
the muffins your girlfriend made
just for you plastic unbreathing blocking
your back from breathing growing an oval
of sweat around itself *Take it*
easy we tell one another as if
there is a way to tell life
I'm taking it easy I have no
time for illness not even
someone else's Maria

is in a different
country My fault the fault
line between us My
travels Chemo radiation their
own country On my way
down the peak I took
another dog's poop—
it was bagged—offered
to take it to the trash
much to the dog's
person's surprise the dog a water-
colour composition of my own
dog's colours wagged
his tongue in response
That's when
the hawk

red-tailed gliding
on time tied it
in a circle

Four Cardinals

Colour of post
storm sky breeze
in mid

afternoon lost
memory it could almost
have disappeared but for the ripple

it made in the earth
coloured water
When asked

the colour of the sky Deutscher's
daughter daughter
of a linguist could not

say What is the colour
of absence? of a wish? of the mind's
reflection? At the block

party we introduced
ourselves by our house
numbers 24 as if

we might be recognized
by the stairs we climb
each day the door jamb

our fingers brush as we try
to remember
what it is we forgot

Alphard
At Deer Lagoon from the neutral
beiges and browns greys

and blacks a blue
stepped beak sharp
as a pick Our worship

built into its name The Great
Blue
Heron swallows

whole its prey has been
known to
choke Its diet

is not limited
to fish and bugs
It will eat mice too

and other birds Tonight
the Worm Moon rises
in the company

of Hydra water snake
largest
of the 88

constellations To the north
a bell ting
tings the 506

Carlton Red flashes
between white-
washed buildings I watch

from this house
where the floors tilt
in every

direction and the arch
over the back
door is mounted up

side down 18's bird
feeder swings A ripple
the colour of

Unframed

In the Vietnamese language, there is no present or past tense. Verbs are not conjugated. Time is discerned through context. Without context, there is no going or gone or will go: you can only be. In my family's photo albums, photos are arranged in no particular order. On the left, my family before a cathedral in Montréal. On the right, my sisters in saris. Falling out of the album, American students marching in support of the war in Việt Nam. About three inches wide with deckle-edged frames, sepia-toned photos of people I don't know but see in my mother's face. My father in a cowboy hat in the desert.

Yesterday's Bread

Some days   fall away

      dry   as paper
              delicious as

Some nights soar
      almost   perfect V-

      formations Now

     someone's sleeping
could be   my neighbour   breath

   like bark   rough-hewn   soothing

to the touch
   Tomorrow   I promise

      will be like   no other

    because   which of us
could   repeat   a performance

   like this one

4

Rules of the Game

It's 1975 Big cats stalk
the TV screen
    bring down
        helpless deer

First the zigzagging
the eternal
        pauses: nervous legs
            twitching wide

eyes blinking Then the narrowing
down the separation
        of the weakest
            from the pack

The relieved
flight of the others—
        white tails
            disappearing

into woods
The lone one heart
        beating fast tired
            of struggle that ends

the same way
every time Still it runs
        It has to These are the rules
            of the game

Imaginary Menagerie

In the end it was
as in the beginning No one
learned anything What was alive
was killed and stuffed
put on display The remaining live
wandered around amongst the dead
wondering what they looked like
when they were alive and in the positions
in which they were now posed which the live
could have witnessed in life
had they not killed
the now
dead

Model Rival: A Lullaby

I too am frequently mistaken
for those only distantly
related to me

I too sing a song
others consider grating
am inclined to hide

found objects I too am viewed
sometimes as a warrior
goddess sometimes

an omen sometimes
an entity of uncleanliness
and deceit depending

I too value a good
twig like to slide
down a snow-

covered hill
I too follow others'
tracks dreaming

Sonnet for a Sharp-Toothed Dreamer

Star of a gnathic nightmare, boasting narrow
snout and jutting lower jaw, scissor
teeth and scaled cheeks, a chain pickerel,
in a serpentine weave, parts a cluster
of weeds, spies a fellow benthic dweller,
a molting crustacean, toboggan down
to the verdant velour bog floor. Patterned
like a rock-lined river bottom, part sun,
part stone, this fork-tailed fan of an ambush
waits behind her aquatic curtain, when
the still soft-shelled crayfish catches the light,
inviting the ensorcelled piscivore
to lunge, prehistoric jaws wide and
dreaming of a gorge of minnows and fry.

Hai: Present (Tense)

In Vietnamese the self cannot be defined
except through its relationship to others

I the younger/older sister maternal/
paternal uncle venerated fe/male elder

In English not even the two tiers
of French

No *tu*
No *vous*
A generic *you*

And *I*
No strings attached
Only country

He saw himself:
a bird soaring

The problem:
the glistening

cage

blue green all endless

like homesickness

Birds
everything they say
is song

Atmospheric River
(collides with migraine)

LA Times article accessed
   4:34 p.m. (PST) *a continuous conga
line of moisture* orographic lift
   mountaintops dancer
gliding one knee
   sunlight glancing
off the glossy
   mugs and glasses silver-
ware and stainless steel
   bowls I have not
washed all day my head
   squeezed a wrung
sponge Vulcan's Fire
   aloe in bloom orange
as an emoji Nature's
   neon River asleep
on the sofa he's not
   supposed to be on (not
my rules) one paw
   tap tapping lands
known only to him pre-
   here pre-animal
shelter He calls
   to a person a bird a
billowing bag flying
   through a field fickle
as this February

5

Ba: Living Room

There are a few things I know—no, believe—to be true. My father's name was Tran Long Nghi. Some of his documents transpose his first name with his last, or his first with his middle.

My mother's name is either Trân Thị Marie or Trần Thị Maria, depending on whether you trust her passport or her other documents. She herself uses both names. On my baptismal certificate, *Juyeng* is written in the space where my mother's name was to be recorded. This is not a Vietnamese or a French name, nor is it a phonetic spelling of one.

Some of my mother's documents list her birthdate as March 1st, some March 13th. My mother's real birthdate is unknown. The passport she used when she immigrated was issued by a country that no longer exists. It lists no month or day, only a year—a different year from the one on her American passport.

My parents' seven children were born in five different countries. Each of us answers to two or three different names. It is unclear how some of the names originated. I do not have a Vietnamese given name. My birth certificate lists my given name as Barbara. Not a single blood relative calls me this.

Inside the family albums are many loose photographs.
On the back of one is a child's hesitant handwriting.
In Vietnamese: *This is the living room.*

The furniture here is found in no other photograph.
It is distinctly Western. And hip for its time, the early
to mid-Sixties. Such furniture could have been bartered
for months' worth of groceries.

A man's hat rests on a mid-century modern
compartmented coffee table, along with what appears
to be a can of beer.

A tripod stretches across a sofa.
The sofa faces two armchairs.
A third chair faces a narrow French door.

It is of a style that could be found in Việt Nam.
There are no people to indicate whether this is Ba's
living room in the United States or Má's in Việt Nam.

The modern armchairs look prohibitively expensive
for a woman raising four children on her own.

They are also too extravagant for a man
new to the United States, sole guardian to two
adolescent daughters. The furniture and the setting
appear to be from opposite sides of the world. I don't
know where I am.

Ba arrived in the United States in 1965.
He was serving as an attaché
to the Vietnamese Ambassador to the United Nations.

This is one account.

Another is that he was
the private secretary to the Foreign Minister.

Another is that he was an accountant.

Whatever the case, he arrived in New York City with his two eldest daughters. They were twelve and thirteen. They arrived in New York City in the midst of the sexual revolution. They were perfect dolls. They posed with their dolls, all four in similar dresses and hats. In the early photos, the girls smile genuinely. They do so even when posed on the beach with women who are not their mother. Their expressions change along with their hair, growing longer, blunter. By the time their mother arrives in New York City, two years later, the eldest has a mod haircut. The other has grown her hair down her back, the way she would have worn it in Việt Nam.

My memory is an album.

The photos are not in chronological order.

Some are out of focus.
Some are bent.
Some may have been placed

in the wrong envelope at the photo-processing lab.

                              In a photo taken in his first
                    apartment in New York City, Ba poses.

He stares directly into the lens.
He was a proud man.
It is a beach chair

                              he lies on
                    in his living room.

The day he died the sky was as clear as a good gemstone.

His inhalations grew shorter and shallower.
He was choking on his own breath.
I measured the morphine with care.
I appreciated that someone thought to dye it
a tranquil blue.

I administered. I watched. I waited.

What comforted was the schedule, the notebook with its
recordings of time and dosage, the dropper with its precise
markings, the aqua blue liquid. These instruments were
my familiars. I clung to them.

$$\left(\begin{array}{c}\text{Horror}\\\text{in the form}\\\text{of awakening and remembering}\end{array}\right)$$

pierced any sleep.

Before and after Ba passed, I scavenged

through the house, collected his photos, spread them out
on my glass desk, first on the west end of Toronto
north of Bloor, now on the east, south of Gerrard.

I have been writing and rewriting this story, re-membering
and furnishing photos of empty rooms, connecting
hairstyles and homes, reaching

for constellations.

There are few photos of Má, even fewer of her
smiling. She is rarely without one of her six children.
Frequently, she is overrun. Not infrequently, she is doing
something for one of them: slicing

birthday cake, squeezing a shoulder to get a child to stand
upright. Sitting is rare. In a few photos, she is trapped in
polite conversation with friends of her husband's. Quickly
she falls out of the frame

the focus remaining on the guests, the children,
the house, the city at large. Her husband, the lens
points elsewhere.

In a Christmas photo, the youngest (at the time) wears stiff denim jeans that make it difficult to squat. He gets smacked for squatting. Ba tells him to act civilized. They are poor but they have chairs. The boy needs to use a fork. The three brothers wear the same style sweatshirt in different colours. It is cheaper this way, and in this way they are marked, if they were not already, with their flat faces and roughly chopped hair.

The boys smile with the rifles they received for Christmas.
They pretend to take prisoners.
They enjoy giving orders.

They enjoy finding their targets, identifying where they will take their charges, considering how they might hurt or frighten them.

When their sister arrives on the scene, the only sister who was left behind with them in Việt Nam, they lay down their guns. Pretend games do not frighten her. Plastic guns mean

nothing. She commands them to get her a Chip-a-Roo from the cupboard. She directs them to chop the carrots their mother instructed her to prepare for dinner. She orders

them to keep their mouths shut. She pinches, twists, strikes, and glares. She does so without hesitation, without having to consider how violence looks. She knows. Even in their best

pretend games, the boys can never approach her unrehearsed acts.

He says he must take the job.
He will be paid handsomely.
They need the money.
It's an important mission.

He leaves. Leaves his wife, who barely speaks English, leaves her with seven children, who speak little English, who are always hungry. Leaves them after they boarded that monstrous machine to be with him again, let go their contact with the earth and water, turned away from family, friends, foes to come to this land. Leaves.

Photos arrive in the mail: him, posed in front of new cars,
beside palm trees, in hats with brims so large they cast
shadows that obscure his face. These brims imply the kind of
sunshine they once knew, the kind they'd prefer to be in
now rather than in the shadows of the tall tower where
they now live. Their mother warns them. There are occupancy
laws in their new home. Their very existence puts them in
violation. She tells her children to hide.

There are no photos where Lady Liberty's face and my sisters'
are visible within the same frame. My sisters are posed only
at Lady Liberty's back. They smile in her shadow.

For his own portrait, Ba stands below a sign with a single word that runs the entire width of the store:

PEERLESS

It is snowing.
The photo is out of focus.
Night is falling.

He will soon be obliterated.

There is a series of photos of me as
an infant, learning to sit up, propped
in a line of dolls. Screaming. The time between this

and when I am walking is un-
documented, is replaced by photos of Ba
standing before a backdrop of cacti, squinting

against the sun and dust. He is well dressed but always alone.
There are houses and vehicles but no people. It is as if he has
alighted in a land that has been abandoned by man.

Who takes the photo?
Who eats dinner with him?
Does he call home?

In the photos at the point in time when I can walk
comfortably, I sport red cowboy boots.

    I wear them in the snow.
    I wear them with dresses.
    I wear them with my hair pulled back in pigtails.

These are snapshots. By virtue of their nature,
at times they distort the truth, slicing
open a moment, snaring

a facial expression on its way
to something else. The framing is
sometimes deliberate, sometimes

accidental. Here, an untied shoe. There,
the whole family,
in size order.

                A stranger appears at the back of this shot.

    My brothers are pushed to the borders in this one.

    This much I know:
        This is the living room.

        But whose?

Interlude

my sisters'
                        laughter   glows
              evening dark lit

       sadness
when the sound
       is prolonged   joy

              when brief
       dust bath forest
              bath bath of bird

              song
equations
       for a rising body

The green corner of a label remains, sticking
teasingly to the cover of the slim address book.
Whatever information the label once imparted
has long since peeled away. Above the green,
the year is embossed in gold: 1975.

Some of the entries inside are so faded they are difficult
to read. A man accustomed to impermanence, Ba
preferred to write in pencil. Many of the contacts listed
are Vietnamese. Most are located in New York, some
in Virginia, a few in Việt Nam.

Recorded on the inside flap—of both the front and back
cover—is Ba's Certificate of Naturalization number.
Was it a reminder that he could no longer return to the
country that he called home for forty-four years? Or, more
practically, was the twice-recorded number a reflection of
his concern, a gesture toward self-preservation? Did he fear
being stopped and interrogated in the only place he could
now call home?

In the middle of the address book is an entry that lists no name, either for an individual or a business, instead tantalizing with a one-word question: *Jobs?* And an address in Rego Park, Queens, New York.

Near this listing is another, more complete. It includes not only a name, address, and phone number, but also a hint after the name, in parentheses: *(private detective).*

A different entry promises *Mexican snacks.*

Another offers almost nothing at all. No contact name, no location, no phone number, not even a city. Its only offering, a reminder of its existence: *Suicide Prevention Center.*

Ba was a self-taught speaker of multiple languages.
Má, like me, fluent in only one (though different ones).

    She can answer none of my most pressing questions.
    She tells me he never had a hair or pencil out of place,
    that he enjoyed taking photographs without any people
    in them and was extraordinarily protective of his plants.

On my desk sit two biographies of a man, not Ba.
I read them as if they might reveal something to me.

And they do. Flagged with Post-its, they surrender secrets
in a manner not so different from the way a person might:

in measured layers, offering facts but withholding
crucial details, repeating certain phrasings, teasing
with ambiguous wording.

The Vietnamese subject of these biographies
grew a moustache to disguise himself
when he went into the field.

He told his colleagues that the women
of Huế preferred the hippie look.

He called himself a doctor of sexology.
He said he was bird watching.

He was, in fact, an intelligence agent.
His mistress was the American occupation.

In the year of the Tết Offensive, Ba left the family
for a job in Texas. He was, he said,

teaching American officers Vietnamese.
He took no family members with him.

In the photos he sent home during this period,
no people other than himself appear. Even

the background is scrubbed
of human presence. It is a desert
literally and figuratively.

Another version of this story:

Ba is planting seeds teaching
    his language

            willing shared words
            to blossom into peace

        A different kind of blossom opens
        Malcolm Browne's photo

            the Buddhist monk
                Thích Quảng Đức

    ablaze Like a flowering
            ocotillo in the desert

                he drew all eyes
        before rejoining

                    the earth

6

Resilient in Rain

Let me say
It's been really difficult

to learn
how to live

from clementine
to cumulus

Once
I thought it was easy

to leap
from daisy

(Gerbera) to dais
But these days
I'm not so sure

If only the most
nectar-

voiced birds sang
who

would be left?
No offense

Not you or I
no starling
no mouse

                    no carnation
                    no spaghetti
                        squash

It would be all
colourless

                diamonds and no
                        buses

   Forget it

I want to keep
my pinecones
my wheelbarrows

                                glazed
                                with rain

How else will I ever learn

                            to find
                    my own feather?

The Art of Armadillidiidae

after Elizabeth Bishop and Jericho Brown

A poem is a gesture toward home
A snail balancing the weight   of its exoskeleton on its soft body

    The weight   of these days on our soft bodies
    Water's lullaby   pulling us ever seaward

We say it as if it's softer than "cancer"   the "C-word"
How many soft bodies   rely on such a flimsy euphemism as a shield

    Conglobation   may serve as a more effective shield
    Take a note   from the Armadillidiidae

who roll up when confronted with pressure   Armadillidiidae
are land crustaceans Their lobster cousins harder   shelled

    During molting they crack their   shields
    straight down the back   leaving them exposed

but for a   paper-thin exoskeleton
enabling them to replace   parts of themselves they've lost

    regrowing lost   legs claws antennae Haven't we all lost
    something in this shell of a year   lost

something we'd like to replace   I lost
my heart my head (lost over some   trifle probably)

I lost my uncle my mother my way By   the laws of probability
the losing's   not over What's left

to do but gather   what's left
of me   *A poem is a gesture toward home*

The Translator: Fire

After the mynah bird's tongue
was split open by the chili
peppers he fed it

>
> after the rough outer layer
> of its tongue peeled
> off

after it finally did
what he
commanded

>
> after the bird gave in and cawed
> *Speak stupid*
> *speak*

morning after morning
Ba would have given anything
to return it to its original ignorant

>
> state Instead day after day
> he was greeted with the same
> stale command he himself

had issued to the bird
Only then did he recognize
his mistake and only now

>
> do the other men
> recognize theirs
> In their eyes Ba sees

bewilderment that he
has been allowed to fly free
in their home *Where*

                is his cage? he knows
                they wonder *Who*
                has let him out?

He longs now
for his wife
to join him to feel

                her body curl
                    into his
        the way certain words

in Vietnamese
charm his tongue
and settle deep

        in his chest

Corvid Vision

one for sorrow

Forty days and forty nights And at last   Ararat
Noah sent Raven forth
Raven did not return
for all Raven needed
was all that remained   death

two for mirth

Raven calls   *Grok*   mocks me   *grok*

how little I   *grok*

three for a funeral

When something is said to come full
circle does this mark completion or make
a new form

an O
through which another
could fly?

When Raven eats
is it meat
or flesh?

four for birth

Say the East Sea is the   womb

Say nước means both   country

and water Say the   water

broke   Say who broke it

five for heaven

Boon of a breeze

carried   a feather

and father

A temporary   assignment   an apartment

a suit and fedora a sub away

six for hell

Dark-eyed   dark-plumed
An unkindness

A conspiracy
A treachery   Once driven

from its   Eastern range
Now making   a comeback

seven for the devil, his own self

Around me all
                    I can see—
        that which is not

            in fact
before my eyes   I try to swipe
        type *moon*

        phase Auto-
correct replaces it
        with *mom*

            passed This morning
            two crows on a rooftop
                Tent rock

                Fairy chimney
                Earth pyramid
                    Alternating   hard

        and soft
            rock   Minerals
                determine

colour Attention

eight for a wish

Hoodoo residue

                    If the shadow
                    of an idea follows

    how clear
                can thought ever run?

How to drop a shadow past?
    Apollo burned Raven black

            (failure to silence a truth)

nine for a kiss

Raven consumes coyote's castoffs

the innards of rodents both large
    and swallowable flies off to shine

before the silver morning moon
    I go home and swallow the ligaments

tendons flesh whole On dragging wing
    I carry fire and blood mother

and father the war they left behind the
    war they wage daily in their own minds

the moon the sun the leaves I want to
    lay across the page the ones I spill like

lies like breadcrumbs like stories for
    some other creature desperate

to believe to weave into a nest
    of yarn and bone one

she can call ~~safe home hers~~ here
    now

ten for a bird you must not miss

Self-portrait as carrion-
eating crow

The dead enter
my body

and not only rise
but sing as they do

I am the colour
of all things

On my one eye
sits the world

Notes

Two books by Jennifer Ackerman, *The Genius of Birds* and *The Bird Way*, vastly enhanced my understanding and appreciation of birds, their habits, and cognitive abilities.

Alex (Avian Language Experiment) (7)
Alex (1976–2007), an African Grey Parrot participated for thirty-one years in cognitive experiments with American scientist Irene Pepperberg. Shown a mirror after being taught names for colours—not including grey—Alex asked of his reflection, "What colour?" To date, Alex is the only non-human animal known to have posed a question using human language.

Loon Song (19)
For all those whose lives have been irrevocably altered by—or lost amid—the astronomical rise in anti-Asian violence in the wake of the 45th U.S. President's insistence on attaching an ethnicity to the coronavirus.

The narrator in Chris Marker's film *Sans Soleil* asserts, "Madness protects, as fever does."

Feelings in A-Minor (22)
Thanks to Cathy Park Hong for her essay collection *Minor Feelings*.

Precedented Parroting (23)
In 1869, "the *Los Angeles News* and *The Los Angeles Star* began running editorials condemning Chinese immigration and attacking the Chinese as inferior and immoral. Unsurprisingly, there was a concomitant increase in racially motivated attacks against the Chinese."
lapl.org/collections-resources/blogs/lapl/chinese-massacre-1871

Charles Siebert. "What Does a Parrot Know About PTSD?" *The New York Times Magazine*. January 28, 2016. nytimes. com/2016/01/31/magazine/what-does-a-parrot-know-about-ptsd.html

Một: Rooted (31)
Italicized text is from Monique Truong's novel *The Book of Salt*.

Teetering Under Telos (39)
Thanks to Alex Hutchinson, whose article on teleoanticipation was the seed that powered this poem: "Covid-19 is like running a marathon with no finish line." *Globe and Mail*. November 21, 2020. theglobeandmail.com/opinion/article-covid-19-is-like-running-a-marathon-with-no-finish-line-what-does

Four Cardinals (43)
As part of an experiment, Alma Deutscher, daughter of linguist Guy Deutscher, was asked, as she was just learning colour names, to ascribe a colour to the sky. "Why Isn't the Sky Blue?" *Radiolab*, May 21, 2012. radiolab.org/podcast/211213-sky-isnt-blue

Imaginary Menagerie (52)
Much gratitude to Chris Marker for his short film *La Jetée*, a deep well.

Atmospheric River (collides with migraine) (57)
Italicized text is borrowed from this article:
"What is an atmospheric river and why should Southern Californians keep their umbrellas handy?" *Los Angeles Times*. November 29, 2019.
latimes.com/california/story/2019-11-29/what-is-an-atmo-spheric-river-and-why-should-southern-californians-keep-their-umbrellas-handy

Ba: Living Room (61)
Names in this poem are written in the form that I believe each person would have chosen.

Resilient in Rain (89)
The red wheelbarrow belongs forever to William Carlos Williams.

The Art of Armadillidiidae (91)
Without Elizabeth Bishop ...
Italicized lines are Jericho Brown's, from his poem "Duplex" in *The Tradition*.

Corvid Vision (95)
"One for Sorrow" is a nursery rhyme with origins in sixteenth century Britain. Traditionally, magpies are counted, but many versions of the rhyme have since sprouted, and in North America crows or ravens are more commonly featured.

The first line excepted, the text in "six from hell" is borrowed from the Audubon's Guide to North American Birds: audubon. org/field-guide/bird/common-raven

Acknowledgements

My gratitude to the editors of the following publications in which versions of these poems appeared, sometimes with different titles:

XConnect ("Rules of the Game"); *Poetry* ("Loon Song"); *Ploughshares* ("Buttercups in Foil on the Windowsill"); *The Paris Review* ("Sonnet for a Sharp-Toothed Dreamer"); *The New Yorker* ("Imaginary Menagerie"); *Michigan Quarterly Review Online* ("Ba: Living Room"); *The Ex-Puritan* ("Raven Takes Wing"); *Cutthroat* ("Unframed"); *Conjunctions Online* ("Teetering Under Telos," "Precedented Parroting," "Feelings in A-Minor"); *Conjunctions* ("Corvid Vision"); *The Cincinnati Review* ("Red O," "Blue from a Distance"); *The Capilano Review's ti-TCR* ("Atmospheric River (collides with migraine)"); *Canthius* ("Yesterday's Bread"); *Blackbird* ("Four Cardinals"); *Bennington Review* ("Resilient in Rain"); *Arts & Letters* ("The Translator: Fire").

The following organizations—and the individuals who run them— have gifted me community, time, space and/or financial support. Not all the works created with their aid made it into these pages, but what is here would not be possible without the earlier works. Thank you: Ontario Arts Council, Millay Arts, MASS MoCA, MacDowell, Lannan Foundation, Hedgebrook, Diasporic Vietnamese Artists Network, Chula, Canada Council for the Arts, Bread Loaf Writers' Conference, Asian American Writers' Workshop.

None of my writing would be possible without my family. To the Trans!

Over the years, countless friends, instructors, and strangers have taught and nurtured me in ways large and small but impactful. Thank you.

To Monique Truong and Loida Maritza Pérez, who have served as beacons from the outset, guiding me and my writing over both troubled and invigorating waters, and to the universe for gifting me their friendship, my deepest gratitude. As well, to these kinfolk: Morgan Ommer, Vinh Nguyen, Marie Myung-Ok Lee, m Burgess.

To my inimitable Writing Cru—Jamie Zeppa, Shelley Saywell, Janet Looker, Debi Goodwin, Maria Coletta McLean, Maria Cioni—for your boundless generosity and wisdom, and for the prosecco: Grazie mille.

Deep gratitude to the members of She Who Has No Master(s) and AfroMundo. Even when you are far, you are near.

Special thanks to Hoa Nguyen, for her lively Sunday poetics classes, where she shared ingredient lists from which a number of poems in this collection were made.

This book would not be without my editor, Jim Johnstone. Thank you for listening to my song, *hearing* it, and guiding me to strengthen it. Thank you to Aimée Parent Dunn, Publisher of Palimpsest Press, for the gift of these pages; Yen Ha, for cover art I might have encountered in my dreams; and Ellie Hastings for bringing this book alive with your keen eye and design.

Four individuals who had not an iota of interest in this book were instrumental in its making. Tomba, Tashi, Sprocket, and River remind/ed me daily that the best poetry is happening right now—probably outside. For keeping my furred beloveds (and by extension, my mind) in good health and spirits, my eternal gratitude to Carolyn Benson.

One person stands at the heart of everything: Bob Gazzale, my love. Who knew an economist could place such great value on poetry?

~

As I write this, our planet has just endured its hottest month in at least the last 120,000 years. This year, in Canada, over 25 million acres have been lost to wildfires, and a month of peak fire season still lies ahead of us. Under these circumstances, what is a meaningful land acknowledgement? (See Cliff Cardinal's *The Land Acknowledgement*.) The best that I can offer in this moment is to pose questions for us to ponder: How much unceded land/sea/air have we taken? How do we, each one of us settlers, begin to take significant and enduring steps toward reparations and responsible stewardship?

About the Cover Artist

Yen Ha is an architect, artist and writer. Born in Saigon, she lives in New York City, where she co-founded the architecture firm, Front Studio. Her short stories appear in the *Bellevue Literary Journal, Waxwing* and the *Minola Review*. Yen has been awarded artist residencies by the Banff Centre for Arts and Creativity, MASS MoCA and the Arctic Circle. Most recently Yen's work was featured on a full-size billboard in New York City as part of the Asians Belong Here public art campaign.

About the Author

Barbara Tran's poetry and fiction have appeared in *The Paris Review*, *The Malahat Review*, and *Conjunctions*. Included in Barbara's writing for the screen is the narration for *Madame Pirate: Becoming a Legend*, a short XR film, which was a 2022 Official Selection of SXSW and in competition at the Cannes Film Festival. Barbara's poetry collection *In the Mynah Bird's Own Words* was the winner of Tupelo Press's inaugural chapbook award. A co-editor of *Watermark: Vietnamese American Poetry and Prose, 25th Anniversary Edition*, Barbara is a member of the *She Who Has No Master(s)* and *AfroMundo* collectives. Much of her writing is conceived while walking, playing, or sharing a tasty morsel with a rescue dog.

In memory of Trần Thị Duyên